CONTENTS

A WALLET FALLS

I was with a friend at a coffee shop. Being kind of thirsty I reach over to grab a coconut water, which caused me to accidentally drop my wallet. "Oops" I say. Of course, it hits the ground square and all my cards pop out making for a minor inconvenience and pretty hilarious episode. I pick up everything and get back up, continuing my conversation. But my friend has changed their demeanor and wasn't really interested in talking too much anymore. They ended up needing to leave for work rather *suddenly* and ... well... *"unexpectedly"*.

"Odd." I think to myself.

Later I found out what happened: A mutual friend of ours called me to explain everything, he let me know that myself and this other friend probably weren't going to be able to be friends anymore. I asked why, and he said she saw one of the cards I picked up and... well... She wasn't too happy about it.

uhhhhh... ok?

You know, it's probably something most of you don't know about me either. What was so offensive? Well, my National Rifle Association card no less. Go figure. I guess it could be worse for my friend, I bet they wouldn't have liked seeing this either:

So there. I guess this is what "coming out" is on the left-coast…
lame. So much emotion, so much <u>misguided anger</u> over this specific subject. So today, I want to talk about the truth of "us". Yeah:
"us". Us "NRA people", and some of the rationale we have.

Fun fact: We're <u>not</u> child-murdering-fascist-racist-homophobe monsters.

Today's story is about: …a perspective, perhaps one that's new to
you, coming from one of America's *most hated* villains: an NRA
member.

:(

Yep.

GROUND RULES

I want to lay down some ground rules to follow throughout this story. It'll serve as a guide for you and help showcase other resources you can look into if you want to discuss further. Plus give some added information about what to expect during your read for today.

1. If you **don't** know me then **I'm going to start by yelling at you for 30 seconds.** Let's just get through it together, and then move on. Ok? Awesome.

2. There are QR codes in quite a few places, these are high-lighting tandem reading material you should look at. Please use your phones camera or tap them to use.

3. I won't be referencing statistics. Yes, all of those anti-gun statistics you've memorized are **laughably incorrect**. If you want to discuss statistics, I'm happy to, but you are required to read Dr. John Lott's gun-control statistics book before we can have a meaningful conversation: Buy the book on Amazon here:

4. I will **not** try to convert you into whatever "cult-of-gun-people" you think the NRA or I am a part of.

5. I **will** explain one perspective pro-gun people have that shows a world where maybe owning and knowing how to use a firearm is a good thing.

So that's where we're at. Trust me, this is as miserable for me as it is you. So let's all take a deep long breath and know that we're all in this *together*.

Cool?

:)

DON'T KNOW ME?

Me: Sigh. "If you don't know me, Hi... My name is PJ, a proud member of the NRA."

You: (some variance(s) of) "Oh my god! One of you MONSTERS!" "WHY DON'T YOU CARE ABOUT THE CHILDREN?!" "Do you NOT care that MILLIONS of people die every year by the hands of evil GUNS!" "YOU ARE DESTROYING OUR MOST VULNERABLE IN OUR NATION!" "RACIST!!" "FASCIST!!!!" "YOU GUN-LOVING MANIAC!!!!!!" etc etc etc...

Ok... Here's my response:

"You are an absolute asshole. You condemn me with zero evidence that I supposedly do not care about children or others who've died as a result of gun violence. To that: Fuck you. You've built a throne of self-righteous evangelical moral superiority that you yourself have chosen to grace yourself in. How *big* of you. You've then decided, in this moral stupor, that you have the god-like authority to judge anyone's soul who disagrees with you as the bearer of all evil itself. And then, you actually *find the audacity* to construct this insanity on the graves of dead children who have died in massacres as some sort of pretentious medal of moral honor, a crown of holiness that promotes your moral judgement actions up to the level of self-appointed god of righteousness: Go fuck yourself, you fucking maniac. We really all want the same things: Safe schools, safe streets, and safe communities for everyone around. It's that we have *vastly* different opinions on how to accomplish this as a nation. *That* is the conversation we need to have that *you* aren't allowing by acting like this fucking spoiled holier-than-thou brat."

Sigh. Can we move on? Great. This all started one day when your system failed me,

This is the story of why I joined the NRA...

HOLD MUSIC

Got off the LA Metro 180 bus a stop too early, it happens from time to time. Usually just shrug it off and figure a little walk is probably good for a bit of exercise. It's Atwater Village for gods-sake, one of Los Angeles's most gentrified and safest east-side neighborhoods. I'm fine. Walk over to the crosswalk for one of our main streets to head back home.

Waiting at the light, and a bit bored, my attention darts around to do a quick awareness check. A couple laughing, walking away from a local bar a bit drunk, cool. The owner of Los Feliz Liquor is outside, sweeping the sidewalk. He's cool. Down the street there's Jack, one of the neighborhood homeless guys, screaming at a blank wall drunk and/or high, ...again, this is normal. He's fine, we'll just leave him alone. A car that's at the intersection, waiting for a green light.... But it's... kind of *out* in the intersection, which is kinda odd. There's a SUV that just pulled up behind it, then seeing that it's in the intersection backs up a bit to give it some room. But the car doesn't move... Ok... The car has pretty heavy window tint, so you can't quite see in. You know what, they probably just aren't paying attention. Pssh, leave it.

Green light.

Cool, start crossing over the street and continue on my journey. While walking over the street I keep checking back in with the odd car, which is a maroon Lincoln sedan, expecting it to suddenly come alive and get through the intersection. It didn't. About halfway over the street is when the first honk from that silver Mercedes SUV happened, the car that pulled up before. I look, but still walk my original route, only to see the maroon sedan hasn't moved an inch... Finally get over to the other side and look back... Wow... Ok... *Now* you can look through the front windshield... There's *no driver*. Uhh...That's *odd*.

BEEEEEEEEEP BE BE BE BE BE BE BE BE BEEEEEEP! Goes the Mercedes.

Red light.

The Mercedes guy has now lost his mind, visually flustered by this maroon sedan. He opened the door a bit, so a light turned on illuminating his arms flailing around and beet-red face. I'm still on the other side waiting for the light to walk back across to investigate. Cars going through the intersection, honking and screaming at this maroon ghost ship that's in everyone's way.

Green light.

Finally! The Mercedes guy immediately slams their door shut

and pulls around the maroon car to jet through the intersection, leaving the scene. Meanwhile, I'm crossing the street, heading directly to this curious sedan to get to the bottom of our mystery.

It's pretty dark out, so you can only really see through the front windshield. Inside the maroon sedan are <u>two unconscious women</u>. ...Wow... Uhhh. Ok. I start tapping, then knocking, then pounding, then *beating* on their car to try to wake them up. One of them would at least *almost* get up, kinda look in my... *guess* you could say: 'direction', then she'd just *lights-out* and collapse, like she'd been drugged. Yikes.

> *Fun fact: I've actually been drugged before. I used to play drums in a hard rock two-piece band with a female lead. At one of the shows over in the Red River district of Austin, some fuck-head decided to drug Kimberly's water that was behind one of the sound stage monitors. Ha! Jokes on him... It was mine. Yeah, getting drugged mega-sucks. It's basically the 'blackout / pass out / I don't remember last night' portion of drunkedness, without the fun drunk part. Plus, super illegal, and super-absolute-fucking-dirt-douche-bag.*

Another car has pulled up behind, two guys got out and approached me. "What's going on?" one of the guys questioned. I *do* have to point out: I *was* beating on this car when they pulled up, so I immediately point inside, "They're unconscious." They start looking when a woman from *their* car yells out, "What's going on?!" "Two girls are passed out!", he says. The girlfriend must have had plans, "I don't care! I'm cold! It's not our problem! Take me home!" The two guys look back at me with a 'we can go right?' look on their face, like I needed to stamp their wrists with a "wasn't-a-terrible-human-being-today" stamp.

I decide to pull my phone out, as my two "friends" here were busy contemplating their lives and how much they were going to allow this incident to mar their evening, to finally put this whole thing to rest and get these two women the help they need **right now. So**...

I call 911.

... annnnnnnnnnnnd **I'm on hold**.

Let's paint this picture: It's around 9pm, on a Friday night. There are two guys who are simply trying to figure out how little they can do, and still *say* they did something. A cold, tired, wants-to-go-home girlfriend, that wants nothing to do with this whole thing. And then there's me, standing in the middle of this intersection, next to a maroon sedan, on the phone... with 911... **on. hold.**

One minute goes by... **still. on. hold**.

A thought came up:

"If I just now called 911 because a serial murderer broke into my place... It is at *this moment*, this *exact <u>moment</u>*, right *{<u>now</u>}* that I would have realized: ***I'm going to die tonight***, and there's ***absolutely nothing*** I can do about it."

15 additional minutes go by... **still. on. hold**. I look, yep those two women are still *very* much unconscious, and I'm still *very* much on hold. A full *16 minutes* into a call with 911, a call to which **<u>nobody</u> <u>answered</u>**, a patrol car going to an *unrelated call* just happened to drive by us. I flagged them down to stop, explained the whole situation and left it with those authorities.

I walk back to the crosswalk dumbfounded. Waiting for a walk light, thinking to myself...

"I find it odd that I'm supposed to depend on this system, a system I've never been allowed to test for its efficiency or <u>if it even works at all</u>. This is my first real use of this system, calling on behalf of these two women who were in dire need of this system working. They <u>expected</u> to have a working system tonight, as did I. We've been told our entire lives to <u>trust</u> this entire system, that it will <u>always</u> be there to save us when we need it most. But here I am, was on the phone... with 911... literally watching the system fail... right in my hand."

So...

For today, let's take a look at some of the other pieces of this *system*. A *system* you might have to depend on at some point, with *your* life...

A POOL PARTY

L et's step back from that 911 call. *Never* actually spoke with anyone, ok... fine. Whatever. Who cares, right? But at least my call was actually routed through my mobile carrier to the 911 emergency call center. At least *that* always works right? We have to be able to count on *that* happening, correct? What kind of telco provider would screw *that* up? I mean... come on... right?

...

Well… actually…

AT&T reaches $5.25M Settlement with FCC

Due to an AT&T corporate IT "clerical error" over 15,000 *actual* 911 calls that were *actually* dialed by consumers never reached a 911 emergency call center. These emergency calling consumers got a voice prompt stating: *the call cannot be completed at this time.* One of these outages lasted over 5 hours and affected the entire United States of America.

Fun Nerdy Facts: AT&T staff put incorrect IP addresses into their whitelist IP pool that's used in network security groups to allow data to and from their emergency call vendors: Comtech and West for subscribers within the United States. That change cut off 911 services as the connections for those 911 calls appeared to be "malicious attacks" on their network segments and they were simply null-routed out of the system.

$5.25M Official AT&T Penalty Order - FCC-DA18-649A1

At least they got caught and fined right? Wow! Imagine that, a giant corporation that will *actually* learn a lesson in this country. Awesome! It's not like AT&T, on the **exact same day** they were fined, would announce an added $1.23 monthly charge to every single one of their global subscribers. Which would, of course, wipe out any ill effects a fine might have on their quarterly profits.

They'd never do that… *right*?

¯_(ツ)_/¯

◆ ◆ ◆

Let's play around a bit, put this into a hypothetical: You're sound asleep one night when CRASH!!!! You pop up looking around, disoriented. "Was that my alarm?" Looking over, the clock says it's 2am. Still confused as to the noise when... THUD!!! Uh-oh... *Something* is happening in the living room... You sneak up to the door peering in, seeing that serial killer maniac I mentioned earlier, coming in through the window. You immediately grab your phone and dial 911, and let's just say you are *actually* able to call, and are *actually* able to get through to an operator, that *actually* picked up. Then, you run into your closet to hide from this maniac.

Now let's say, for whatever reason, you're able to *fully* talk and able to *freely* and *clearly* give your correct address and *completely* explain what is going on, all while hiding for your life in the closet. And then: let's just say, for whatever reason, that this 911 operator actually types in your correct address and info to get it over to dispatch right away. Ok! Here we go! Now we have a police officer on the way! Now we're going to be safe, right?

...

...*right?*

TO PROTECT AND
...wait a minute

Once the police show up, they have to *protect* you, right? I mean, that is their *job*. All of their cars and vehicles say: "To *Protect* and Serve", so we should be able to safely assume that *protecting people* is a core part of their *job*, right? That is their *job*, correct? *Protect people*?!

Right?!

...

Well... not exactly...

The Story of Jessica Lenahan (Gonzales)

I guess you could say Jessica and Simon had a fairly typical start to their marriage. Met each other while attending High School in Pueblo, Colorado. Married each other in 1990, ended up having three daughters together, Rebecca, Katheryn, and Leslie. Jessica also had a son, Jessie, from a previous relationship.

But things were not all they could be, throughout their marriage Simon would be erratic and abusive towards both Jessica and the kids. And as the years wore on, so did the abuse and violence. This really came to a head in 1994 where Simon was really distancing himself, becoming more controlling, unpredictable, and violent. By this point Simon was heavily involved in drugs, breaking everything, harshly disciplining the kids, threatening to kidnap them, driving recklessly, talking about committing suicide, plus verbally, physically, and sexually abusing Jessica.

After the family moved to Castle Rock, Colorado in 1998, things did not improve.

One day Jessica walks into the garage, to find Simon with a noose around his neck attempting to hang himself ... oh... *and* the kids were watching. Jessica desperately pulls the rope away from his neck, while Leslie (the daughter) called the police.

Finally, in 1999, Jessica and Simon separated. But Simon couldn't stay away, he started stalking Jessica inside and outside the house, at her work, and call her at all hour's day and night.

On May 21, 1999, a Colorado court granted Jessica a temporary restraining order that required Simon to stay at least 100 yards away from Jessica, all of her children, and the house. The judge in that case told Jessica to keep the order with her at all times, and that the order and Colorado law required the police to arrest Simon if he violated the order.

But Simon just couldn't stay away, he continued terrorizing Jessica and the kids, repeatedly breaking the restraining order. He broke into their home, stole jewelry, changed the locks on the doors, opened up water valves on the house. All sorts of nonsense. Jessica would repeatedly call the police, to which they would *promptly ignore*. In the rare event they'd actually respond, they were dismissive of her, even scolding her for *calling at all*.

Meanwhile, Simon is having his own issues with the law. Ticketed for road-rage with the daughters in the bed of the truck during his weekend with them. Another he was caught trespassing in a private section of the *actual* Castle Rock Police Station. And yet another for fleeing police after officers served him with said restraining order.

June 4th, 1999. Both Jessica and Simon appeared in court and the judge made the restraining order permanent. The new order was quite strict, Jessica had full custody of their daughters, and Simon could only see them on alternate weekends and one prearranged dinner visit during the week.

Then... 3 weeks later: June 22nd *happened...*

- 5:15pm
    - Simon kidnaps Rebecca, Katheryn, and Leslie from the front yard of the house.
- 5:30pm
    - Jessica notices the kids missing, calls the police to report that Simon had broken the restraining order.
        - Police dispatch says they are sending an officer to their house.
            - No officer ever came.
- 7:30pm
    - Simon attempts to purchase a handgun and ammuni-

tion.

- Police *forgot* to report the restraining order into NICS (National Instant Criminal Background Check System)
  - Because of the omission, Simon is approved for purchase.
- Jessica calls the police again, demanding a police response.
  - Police send two officers. Jessica shows them the protective order which clearly shows today is not a day Simon is allowed to see the kids.
    - Police tell Jessica: "Well he's their father, it's okay for them to be with him." Then tell her there's nothing they can do, but to call back at 10pm if they still aren't back.
- 8:15pm
  - Simon's current girlfriend calls Jessica. Tells Jessica that Simon was threatening to drive off a cliff.
  - She then asks Jessica if Simon had a gun and whether or not he would hurt the children.
- 8:30pm
  - Jessica is finally able to get Simon on the phone, he tells her they are at Elitch Gardens amusement park in Denver.
  - Jessica immediately calls the police to give them this information.
    - Police tell Jessica: "That's outside of our jurisdiction." Then mentioned this needed to be taken to divorce court. One officer told Jessica: "At least you know the children are with their father."
- 10:10pm
  - Jessica calls the police again
    - Police dispatch tells Jessica that she's being "a little ridiculous making us freak out thinking

the kids are gone."

- 12:00am
  - Jessica drives to Simons apartment. He wasn't there. So she calls the police again.
    - Police dispatch ask the following questions: "How many children are missing?", "What are their names?", and "How old are they?" Dispatch promises another officer.
      - No officer ever came.
- 12:15am
  - Jessica drives to the police station and grabs an officer demanding they find her daughters right now.
    - This police officer, who just now spoke with Jessica, then went out for a 2 hour dinner and never attempted to contact Jessica again.
- 3:25am
  - Simon's current girlfriend calls Jessica. Tells her she was on the phone with Simon when she heard gunshots.
    - She tells Jessica that she believes Simon and her daughters are dead.
- 3:20am (5 minutes earlier)
  - Simon drives to the police station and started shooting with the handgun purchased earlier.
    - The police unload a volley of rounds into his car, killing Simon.
      - The three children were found in the trunk, all of them are dead.
      - The police have never spoken to when the children were actually murdered, nor has there been any investigation as to that timing or the circumstances of their deaths.

Honestly, I can't do this story real justice, maybe you should read what Jessica herself said to the Inter-American Commission of Human Rights about what happened that fateful day.

So... Jessica decided to bring a case against Castle Rock Police Department for, I don't know, pretty much *everything* you just read. Makes sense right? Well, that has its own blowback. Her co-workers told her that she must have done something to deserve it. Others simply scolded her for being "money-hungry", while other *others* would just walk up to her pointing "You're that mother!" Her closing thoughts pretty much sum it up:

> ## "I've lost all faith in my government, in the law, and in humanity."
> --Jessica Lenahan (Gonzales)

Oh, but that case, that's something right? ... Yeah... She ended up *losing* that case, and many *many* **many** after. Finally arriving at our nation's highest court, the Supreme Court of the United States, who in 2005 delivered their ruling on Castle Rock v Gonzales, with a 7/2 majority: ... You ready for this? ... Here's a *taste* of what she was in for...

Castle Rock v Gonzales (Majority | S:B P:9)

"Even if the statute could be said to have made enforcement of restraining orders "mandatory" because of the domestic-violence context of the underlying statute, that would not necessarily mean that state law gave respondent an entitlement to enforcement of the mandate. Making the actions of government employees obligatory can serve various legitimate ends other than the conferral of a benefit on a specific class of people."

…Yeah, you read that right:

Police have no obligation to protect you.

Look, the police play an important role in law enforcement, that is the enforcement of laws and penalties for crimes *after* they have been committed. They are not bound by any Hippocratic oath (…*or actual law*) to protect you or your loved ones *before* that event at all.

Fun fact: Law enforcement, including the FBI, were warned multiple times before the Parkland school shooting, Broward County Sheriff's Department was warned 39 times by themselves.

It's a hard thing to talk about, but the people who die at the failing of a system they *think* is in place don't get to tell their side of the story. While the rest of us keep being told that this status quo system works just fine. The status quo system is built to retain *order and compliance en masse*, your singular-personal living or deadness is not a factor of concern here.

Really think about that. Unless the *murder* __rate__… or any other crime __rates__ are going up, nobody frankly gives a crap about you. Your murder is just another statistic the police detectives *now* get to solve! *Congratulations, __#635__*! Everyone *wins*!

Fun fact: There were 634 homicides in Los Angeles over 2018.

Want another story? Cool! Let's get *silly* with this one…

lighten the mood a bit.

Let's set the stage in a NYC subway car. There's a guy sitting in there, that's our victim. He gets attacked by a crazed knife-wielding drugged-out maniac... Ok. You know what? Let's make that maniac a serial killer, killed 4 people the night before, stabbed several more. Ok... check it: let's *really* get ridiculous. Let's add two NYPD officers in the same car... and get this: Let's say the two officers have already identified this maniac as the actual serial killer that they are *specifically* on the train to apprehend. And let's also put them behind a sliding door, you know: Watching this dude viciously attack our victim to which neither of them does a god-damn thing about. Our victim, who isn't a fan of getting stabbed, wrestles the serial killer to the ground, meanwhile getting multiple stab wounds in the head, arms and hand. Our victim, *not the police...* who are *literally standing and watching 6 feet away*, is somehow able to disarm the killer and hold him down. It is at *this* point; the police *finally* open the door to come out and take credit for capturing the maniac, all while completely ignoring our bleeding victim who is in dire need of medical attention. They decide to go ahead and take the serial killer away in handcuffs, while our victim-hero losses conciseness in a pool of his own blood.

Is *that* ridiculous enough?

Well, that's *exactly what happened:*

Watch the Video:

Oh, and NYC followed up with this: City says cops had no duty to protect subway hero who subdued killer. Classy. Go New York! The two cops were also given commendations for their "heroic" (...I wish I was kidding) work in *catching* the killer. Way to go guys! Go team awesome!

It's as hilarious as it is ridiculous.

¯_(ツ)_/¯

Ok, let's go back to our hypothetical from earlier. Serial murderer broke into your place. You call 911, and are *somehow* able to actually get through, and there is, for whatever reason, someone there to *actually* take your call. You are, *again*... however you want to make this up, able to *freely* and <u>*very clearly*</u> speak, while hiding in a closet from someone who wants to *murder you*. You are, somehow, able to give this operator your *correct* location (note: 911 <u>cannot</u> read your GPS!) and *perfectly* tell them what is going on. This operator, *let's just say*, is then able to *correctly* get all of this information into the system and then *immediately* send your call over to dispatch.

Let's just go ahead and say <u>*all of that*</u> is true.

Alright! Dispatch!!! They **now** have your correct information! Ok, you know what? Let's make this ***<u>super-crazy-ridiculously-easy</u>***, they look up on the grid and see an actual officer that's 2 doors down from where you're currently at! Alright! You know what? I'll give you even <u>*another gimme:*</u> This officer is the most dedicated officer in the entire municipal police department. Let's just call this cop "**<u>SUPER COP</u>**!". Super cop takes the call and hauls ass over to your place to save your butt! Now we're *<u>finally</u>*

gonna get saved! Super cop is **on their way**!!!

A SHOT IN THE DARK

Uh-OH!!! Back at your place!!!! **PHRAP**!!!! The maniac throws open your closet accordion doors, finding you buried in the back! He gives a slight smile, "Hi there." But just right then: **CRASH**!!!!!!!!! Your door flies open. It's **SUPER-COP** kicking the door in!!!! Sidearm pulled, super cop is screaming, "**DROP THE WEAPON NOW!!!**" But the assailant isn't complying. Again… "**DROP THE WEAPON NOW!!!! DO IT NOW!!!!!**" You see the intruder clinch that 8" knife even tighter. Super cop brings up their sidearm to take aim… "**DO IT NOW**!!!!" You're behind the maniac, in the closet curled up on the floor...

You're safe *right*?

We trust these officers enough to put loaded handguns in their hands and put them on the streets as law enforcement. I mean, they'd have to be the greatest shooters in the world, *right*? They have to be absolute experts with those firearms! You can't sit there and begin to question this... *I mean...* They obviously must have the most *qualified trainers* and *strictest standards* of anywhere on Earth, *correct*?! Seriously?!

Come on!!!!

...

Well... not really...

About a year ago I was talking with some friends and the subject turned into guns and gun-control. One of *those* friends immediately went off on the NRA and... well, you can *assume* where that conversation went. I just offered back that the NRA is actually a rather established training and safety organization and quite good at what they do.

They laughed... *not* shocking.

But then they came back with this: "Really?! *{laughing}* Ok. So how many of these "safety" classes have you gone to?". Oh... "Uhh... well... I mean I haven't actually... gone, but I've heard really good things..." ... Yeah Peej, you lost that round, give it up. When I went home, I said: You know what? That's fair. So I researched and found an NRA "Basics of Pistol Shooting" class to experience just how good their established training (and/or "safety") classes really are.

So I went.

Let me be clear about this: This was the NRA's *basics* of pistol shooting. Not advanced... not expert... the *basics*. What the NRA has determined as the minimum requirements a person (civilian) needs to safely operate a pistol: The NRA *minimum* standards for *civilians*.

So I completed the class.

> *PJ Fun Fact: Maybe it's noteworthy, maybe not. I'm a native Texan, who grew up on a ranch. So, as you might guess, I've been around firearms my whole life. Shot my first rifle (.22 single shot bolt action) when I was 6, and both semi-auto rifle (.22 Ruger 10/22) and shotgun (20 gauge Winchester semi-auto) around when I was 8. This is normal in rural Texas, in fact... It's quite strange if you haven't fired a firearm before you're 10 there. I wanted to say this to add the following: If you were to come up to me and say that I should go to a firearms class, I probably would have just laughed at you: But because of that conversation before, I decided to go since I totally got called out. At the conclusion of the NRA class, I found myself stunned by how instantly applicable the course content was, and found around 75% the material as 'new' information. I walked out a substantially better and more responsible shooter and could not thank the NRA more for creating such a fantastic course.*

Had a really good time. But now I needed to compare my experience to something to gauge how valuable the course content really is. We have a shooting qualification in the class, which is the practical test of the course content. So I decided to look for state-issued officer minimum shooting qualifications as the benchmark.

So I googled around... and found one.

I found the State of California P.O.S.T. (Commission on Peace Officer Standards and Training) the California state agency that sets the minimum course of fire shooting standards that all armed peace officers in the state must qualify. Here is their training qualification document (it's near the bottom). Again: This is the official set of standards the *State of California* has decided are the *minimum requirements*: The State of California *minimum* standards for *armed officers*.

I grab some targets and head to the range.

Let's start with...

Ok... Interesting... Got it. Now let's check out the NRA targets...

Interesting...

You know what... We might be missing something, how they grade the qualifications can vary quite a bit. Maybe that'll shed some light on this.

Let's go back to the State of California P.O.S.T. and check out the scoring...

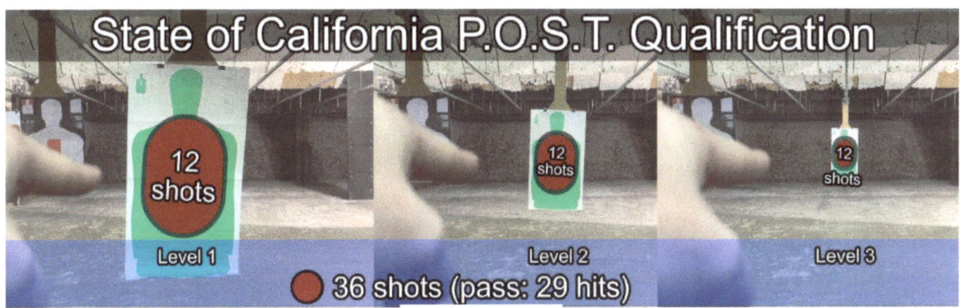

Ok, that's pretty interesting...

So now let's compare this to the National Rifle Association's *Basics* of Pistol Shooting class qualification. Again, this is the *State of California*'s own minimum shooting qualification that all <u>armed officers</u> in the state must qualify, being compared to a <u>civilian</u> shooting organization's ***basic*** *pistol* <u>class</u>:

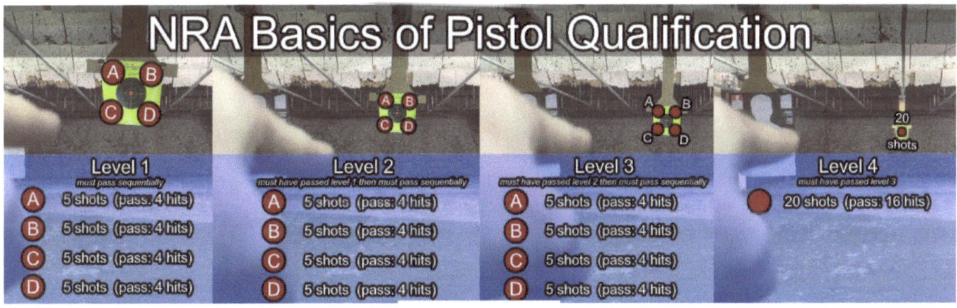

...

Sigh. Well then...

Round fired by officer killed Trader Joe's Store Manager

- Officers decided to fire upon a suspect, who was running into a *very busy* Trader Joe's. Manager exits out of the... *"exit"*, and promptly gets killed.

Sheriff's sergeant was fatally shot by friendly fire

- Officer was shot by another officer's AR15. Sherriff says the accident was: "unavoidable"... *Really*? *"**un**"*-avoidable? So... It ***had*** to happen?!!

NYPD officer accidentally shot himself in the hand

- Officer, while at the PSA1 Coney Island station shot his own hand. I guess playing around with a loaded handgun will do that.

Officer's shooting of partner called accidental

- Officers responding to a home arrest. Homeowner releases a dog, officer attempts to stop dog with hand, ends up shooting their partner instead.

Officer accidentally shoots himself while looking at a handgun

- Officer is at a store looking at a .38 semi-auto handgun. Officer actually cycles the handgun, *then* pulls the trigger... Boom.

Police officer accidentally shoots 4-year-old child

- Family dog races up to a police officer who arrived on scene. Cop shoots at dog... *misses*... ends up hitting their 4-year-old daughter instead.

DEA agent shoots himself during firearm instruction class he was teaching

- Actual quote: "I'm the only one in this room who's professional enough, that I know of, that can carry a Glock 40." Then... <u>*literally*</u> shoots himself.

73-year-old librarian shot dead by cop accidently during gun demonstration

- Officer was role-playing a bad-guy at a demonstration, fired his gun at the librarian... *Oops*. Well... it was *supposed* to be loaded with blanks.

... Or how about one that's more in line with our hypothetical? The one where super cop just showed up to save you from that serial murderer? How about a story where three LAPD officers fatally shoot a hostage in a barrage of bullets from 9 feet away?

So… you **woke** yet?

…because *I am.*

LAST CALL

"**L**ast Call!" screams out the bartender. A densely packed bar in the lower east side of Manhattan after a rather eventful evening. The bartender told stories of New York back when he was a kid and how much of the city has changed. A large group of us were glued to the performance behind the counter as he was walking us through all the years and the full cast of characters that have come throughout his life. Spellbound by the performance, I completely lost track of time, and *maybe* how many drinks I've had. Closed out my tab, and said goodbyes to my new friends while attempting to find the front door...

Finally finding my way outside, and quite disoriented, I start aimlessly walking around looking for any signs of the subway. That's when this man approached me, a friendly stranger...

"You looking for the subway?"

I remember nodding vaguely. This new friend navigated me down some side streets where I started noticing a lot fewer people and a lot fewer street lights.

Finally, we come to a stop...

Tick!

Sounded like a ball-point pen but with more force, I blinked my eyes and that's when I saw it: a knife. Frozen standing there, never taking my eyes off of the weapon while in quite an inebriated state. A deafening silence while my *'friend'* patted me down taking my wallet and phone, then shoved me to the ground before taking off into the night.

A Brief Mugging: The Story

That was in December 2015. The above story is where I talk about the *good* things that actually happened in the ensuing 18 hours. However, *today* I bring up a *bad* thing: What the NYPD sent me 3 months later.

Grabbing my mail I saw a letter from the NYPD, thinking it was actually something about the case and maybe they actually found the guy or phone or something. Who knows, I was just being overly optimistic. So I rip it open, sigh... I had to read this twice:

> *"The NYPD takes all crimes seriously. We would like you to know that your case has been fully processed and has been logged into our annual crime reports."*

So the NYPD sent me a letter letting me know that I've *literally* become a statistic. Wow.

What really bothered me about the whole letter was its own self-congratulatory tone. Like a "Oh, good news for you! Look at all the work we did! We made charts and reports that you're in!" Like I care that my name is briefly mentioned on the closing credits, a feature film: *NYPD Rocked 2015*! Closing you out of the cast knowing that they're done with it, and don't you expect any more effort put into your case. *"Justice"* taking a more *"broader-picture"* viewpoint, where of course I don't see any results but maybe 20 years from now and 1,000s of incidents later they finally grab "The EastSide Mugger!" Yeah... #NotImpressed.

Maybe I just trivialized that incident to the NYPD itself, never fully seeing there was anything else to look into. But that 911 call, that snapped that NYC story right back to the surface, causing me to peel apart pieces of this system questioning it. And at the conclusion of this questioning, I'm left with this:

So...

I am expected to **trust my life** to a system that...

- I may or may not even *be able* to call...
  - Who may or may not *even pick up*...
    - Who may or may not send an officer that has *zero obligation* to protect me or my loved ones...
      - Who is not even held to the same standards as a *civilian shooting organization?*

I'll **use** the system, but I **will not depend** on it.

◆ ◆ ◆

I was never really an active "pro-gun" guy before. I was comfortable with them, grew up around them, but certainly thought NRA people were a bit *much*. "The police were there to take care of us, and that the system worked for everybody. What are all of these crazy gun-loving maniacs screaming about?" … I thought.

Wow. How a story can change your life.

I started telling others what I learned. And to my surprise, that same *scary* NRA group were the only ones that understood what I was saying. In fact, most of the ones I spoke with all had very *very* similar stories. The more I talked… the more they spoke, and then… *here's the important part*: the more I *listened*.

Met up with a friend to get his story…

> *"It was really early in the morning and the alarm went off. It's just my wife and me in the house. Thank god it was the cat, but I realized that if it was an actual intruder that wanted to hurt us, we would be dead. We were not prepared for that."*

Met up with another at a local pub, after a long talk she told me her story…

> *"Ok.. 6 years ago this guy raped me twice in one night. He's a lawyer, so he knows what to do to stall the case, so hasn't even really started. I have to go back there to do court stuff but had to move since he's so dangerous. Cops didn't do a damn thing to help."*

Met another at the range, he ran a pet store here in Los Angeles...

"There was this group of thugs running around robbing shops like mine, heavily armed. They'd smash in while you were closing, tie you up and beat the shit out of you... If you were lucky... They almost killed one guy. Cops told us, 'Just do what they say and hope for the best.'... Nah man, that's ridiculous."

◆ ◆ ◆

Story after story...

What us NRA members call:

Common Sense

◆ ◆ ◆

That walk home was me finally waking up from the mirage of what we're told to believe. A reality, hidden in plain sight. It was my *red pill* of truth.

I got *woke* from the status quo talking-points to see the system for what it really is. Got behind the curtains for once and gasped at a system *full* of faults. Watched decades of promises shatter, a thin veneer of misconceptions to expose the core of *truth*. A *truth* that millions continue to put their lives in the hands of every single day. And the more down the rabbit hole I went, the larger the misconceptions I would find.

Today?... is *your* red pill day.

Or... I guess you can keep taking the blue pill, and just *hope* this system will never fail you or your loved ones. Hope... That day when you *need* this system the most.

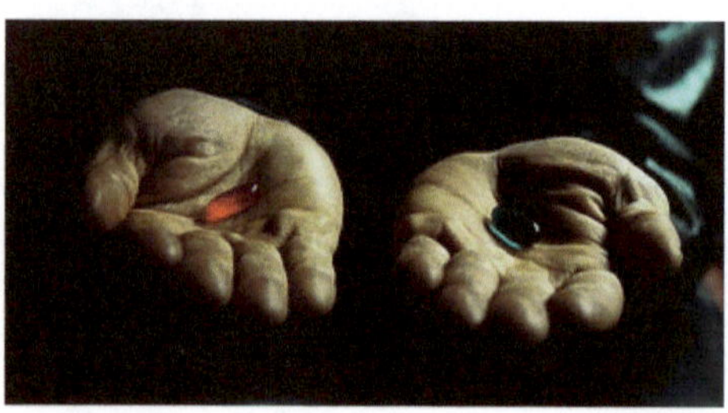

It's *your* choice.

Regardless, I want to thank you for reading and the time you've given me today. You might have a better understanding of us NRA members not as the monsters you're told of, but as the loving rational human beings that we truly are.

And as we begin to wrap up for today, I wanted to leave you with three asks:

- **Talk with us**

We actually really enjoy talking about this subject and answering all of your questions. You don't know what you don't know, and that isn't going to change until you start asking us.

- **Go take a class**

A great and safe way to just be in our shoes for a day. Go take that same NRA Basics of Pistol Shooting Class that I did. I now even, along with *many* other instructors, teach this to people just like you.

- **Listen**

Ask us to tell our stories, they are deeply personal and really get at the heart of why we are NRA members. Again, we are *loving rational human beings...* **Just like you**.

...I love you all,

AN EPILOGUE

Ok! Everyone, thanks for sticking in there! Really appreciated. Now just something I'd want you to know, and two things I really would like you to leave here with...

A Thank You...

First off, I really want you to know how much I appreciate the time you've given me to read through this today. I'm deeply grateful for the open-mind and open-heart you've shown. We're all good people, and having these difficult conversations is how we heal and grow as communities, cities, states and as a country. Thank you for being here and listening.

Cops aren't Gods...

People in law enforcement are beautiful amazing *fallible* human beings just like you and I. They aren't cloned from some engineered DNA of "perfect police officer". They make mistakes, which is fine, as long as they are held accountable for their actions.

Like all jobs on *Earth*, some officers are incredibly devoted and amazing at what they do, and some... well... *aren't*. Some cops will put themselves into a hostage situation, and ultimately die, to save a stranger. As another cop might turn into the Golden State Killer. Putting on a badge doesn't rid a person of making mistakes, crimes, or worse.

It's a job, a career, and to many a great source of pride. As communities, if we could understand that, we might be able to pick up *some* of the personal responsibility. It'd help make their jobs *infinitely* easier and we'd be *significantly* safer, which I'm sure everyone could appreciate.

The Truth...

Finally!! Ok... This *really* could be its own article, but I feel it's immensely important for you to take away with: The "*truth*". I hear a lot now about "**my truth!**" Ok. There is no singular more cancerous thought in the human experience than that phrase. Nobody '*owns*' the truth. It's not something you can pick up, nor hold in your hand. If you ever hear this, visually get a paint scrapper and scrape as deep as you can to rip it out of your brain. Then, to whomever you heard this non-sense, correct them with: "Oh… you mean **your perspective.**"

Look, we're all in a giant dark room with flashlights of *perspective.* In the center of this giant room is a huge complicated structure that nobody is allowed to touch: That's actual *perfect* "truth", hidden in the darkness. You only get to see what your flashlight of *perspective* sees, and the <u>only way</u> to know more of what this *truth* looks like is to <u>share</u> your flashlights *perspective* <u>with others</u>.

It's *not* possible to know perfect truth, that would require infinite perspectives on a specific location of '*the truth*'. The best you can hope for is amassing many *many <u>many</u> <u>different</u>* perspectives of this location, to a point where you think, "ok.. I think I kinda got a pretty good idea of what this thing looks like from a lot of *different perspectives.*"

The phrase "**my truth**!" is cancerous to a society, since it's an idea that *your* individual flashlight of *perspective* is total <u>absolute truth,</u> god-almighty. All *other perspectives* that don't adhere are <u>absolutely false</u> on their face since they are different than your "<u>*absolute truth*</u>" original. This *perspective* has now become <u>a religion of thought</u> as it is now gospel with the believers, and anything that might argue against it is <u>absolute heretic</u> and ***must*** *be destroyed at all costs.*

> Perhaps that sounds like a political conversation you've had recently.

Your *perspective*(s) are amazing and very real, and you should absolutely share them with others. Only through that process will we grow as a people. All it requires is for people to *share* and <u>listen</u> to all of these amazing *perspectives* others have.

It's in that where we have the real American spirit, our innate ability as a country to *learn* and *better* ourselves from the lessons of others. It's *that* which makes us *truly* <u>exceptional</u>.

> ***That*** is ***truly*** **<u>American</u>**.

Really, I love you all.
Thank you again,